Shelly
Goes to the
Zoo

by Kentrell Martin

illustrations by Marc Rodriguez

To the Reader

Throughout the book, Shelly's hands demonstrate how each highlighted word is signed. You will find an alphabet chart at the end of the book. A DVD that provides live interpreter guidance is also available from Shelly's Adventures LLC.

Available now:
Shelly's Outdoor Adventure
Shelly Goes to the Zoo

Coming soon:
Shelly Visits Washington, D.C.
Shelly Babysits her Baby Brother
Shelly Goes to the Dentist

Shelly Goes to the Zoo by Kentrell Martin
Also in the Shelly's Adventures Series: Shelly's Outdoor Adventure

Copyright © 2013 by Kentrell Martin

ISBN (hardcover): 978-0-9851845-3-7
ISBN (softcover): 978-0-9851845-1-3
Library of Congress Control Number: 2012902759

First printed in 2013. Reprinted in 2015, 2017 and 2018.

Published by Shelly's Adventures LLC, PO BOX 2632, Land O Lakes, Fl 34639 USA
Website: www.shellysadventuresllc.com

Printed and bound in the USA

Book design by Jill Ronsley, www.suneditwrite.com

Shelly's Adventures LLC was created to provide children and their parents with reading material that teaches American Sign Language. Shelly's Adventures LLC produces materials that make signing fun for kids, parents and teachers.

"Maria and Kasey, have you been to the zoo before?" says Shelly.

"No," says Maria, "I have never been to the zoo before."

"Me neither! I don't know what to expect," says Kasey.

"Well, you can expect to see many different animals. I'm sure you will enjoy them all," says Shelly as she signs ANIMAL.

Hands pivot towards each other.

The first animal they see is a bear.

Maria looks at the bears' exhibit and says, "Wow! Those are big bears!"

Kasey can't say a word. He just stands there with his mouth gaping.

"Yes, Maria. Bears are big furry animals that can be found in North America, South America, Asia and Europe," says Shelly as she signs BEAR.

Cross arms over chest and claw twice.

They keep exploring the zoo. At the next exhibit, Kasey says, "I know what this animal is! It's the king of the jungle!"

Maria asks, "Where do these animals live, Shelly?"

Shelly says, "Lions live in Africa and Asia. They are the second largest living cat after the tiger." She shows them the sign for LION.

Pull hand backward over head.

Shelly replies, "Kasey is imitating those monkeys on the branches. Monkeys live in trees in the grasslands, mountains and forests and on the high plains. They can be found in almost every country in the world." She shows them the sign for MONKEY.

Scratch your sides twice.

The children move on to the next area.

Shelly points at the striped animal and says, "Look! There is the tiger—the largest living cat. You can tell it's a tiger by the black stripes on its body." She shows them the sign for TIGER.

Make clawing motion back on the face.

Maria says, "His teeth look so big and sharp!"
Kasey smiles and says, "He is looking at me
as if he wants to eat me for lunch.
I'm afraid of him. Let's go!"

They continue to wander through the zoo, wondering what the next animal will be.

Suddenly, Kasey stops and holds his nose.

"Ewwww! Do you smell that?" he says.

Maria frowns and says, "Yes! What is that horrible smell?"

Shelly holds her nose with one hand and points with the other hand at a group of elephants.

Shelly says, "Those are African elephants. They can live for sixty to eighty years. They are endangered due to illegal poaching by hunters and the loss of their natural habitat by land developers."
She shows them the sign for ELEPHANT.

Move hand down and out.

They walk into a cave, and when they reach the end, they see large glass tanks.

Kasey stops in front of the first window and says, "These animals know how to dance. They are moving their head from right to left." Kasey imitates the animals, moving his head from right to left.

Maria laughs and says, "Kasey, you are so silly."

Shelly says, "Those are snakes. The one that is moving its head is a cobra. They live in Asia and Africa. Cobras are very dangerous." Shelly shows them the sign for SNAKE.

Slither your hand forward like a snake.

They watch the snakes for a few more minutes and move on to the next tank. This one is an aquarium, and it's full of fish.

"Wow! I didn't know there were so many different kinds of fish in the world," says Maria.

"Me neither," says Kasey. "Look at the fish with the big mouth at the back of the aquarium."

Shelly says, "There are over twenty-five thousand kinds of fish in the world. That one is called a grouper." Shelly shows them the sign for FISH.

Move hand back and forth.

"Look at those turtles!" says Shelly when they stop in front of the next tank. "Did you know that turtles are reptiles, and they can live up to a hundred and fifty years, or even longer?"

Maria replies, "Wow!
That is very old."

Kasey says, "That is older than
my grandmother!"

Everyone laughs.

Shelly shows them the sign for TURTLE.

Cover hand and move thumb side to side.

Kasey walks ahead of the girls to the next exhibit. Before they catch up, he turns and races back to them.

"I don't think you want to go that way!" he says, out of breath.

"Why not?" says Maria.

Kasey says, "There is a huge animal with a bunch of enormous teeth lying in there."

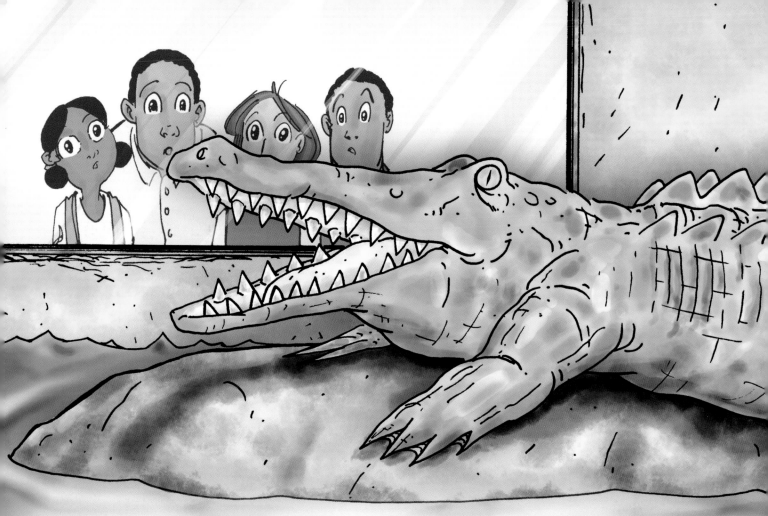

The girls do want to see, and they rush to the next window. Inside they see an alligator lying on a rock with his mouth wide open.

"That's an alligator," says Shelly. "Alligators are reptiles, and they live for about forty years. That alligator has his mouth open because that's how he cools off when he's hot or warms up when he's cold."

Shelly shows her friends the sign for ALLIGATOR.

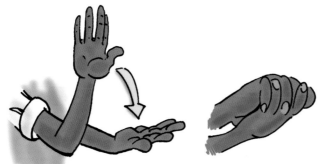

Open and close
hands.

"Let's come back to the zoo another day and visit more animals," says Maria. "Yes," says Shelly, "and I will show you more signs for the animals."

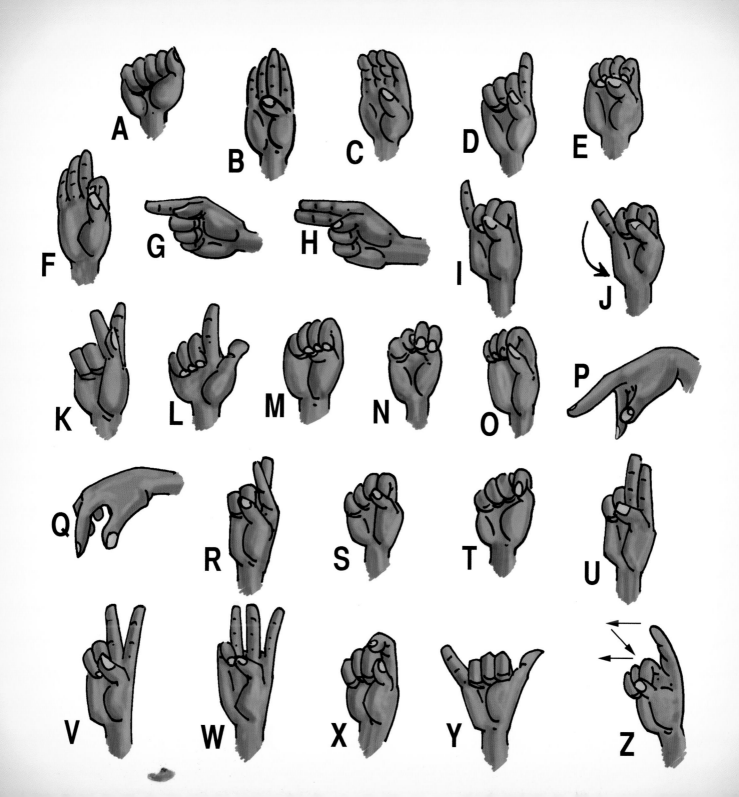